# EATS, SHOOTS & LEAVES

## WHY, COMMAS REALLY *DO* MAKE A DIFFERENCE!

by
**LYNNE TRUSS**

illustrated by
**BONNIE TIMMONS**

G. P. PUTNAM'S SONS

**A** panda walks into the library. He eats a sandwich, then draws his bow and shoots two arrows.

"Why did you do that?" asks the librarian as the panda walks toward the exit.

The panda shows her a badly punctuated book. "I'm a panda," he says. "That's what it says we do."

The librarian looks at the page:

**PANDA**
Large black-and-white bear-like mammal, native to China. Eats, shoots and leaves.

# INTRODUCTION

Punctuation marks are the traffic signals of language: they tell us to slow down, notice this, take a detour, or stop.

Of all the punctuation marks, the comma is the most used and misused. Commas can create havoc when they are left out or are put in the wrong spot, and the results of misuse can be hilarious. This little dot with a tail has the power to change the meaning of a sentence by connecting things that shouldn't be connected or breaking apart things that should stay together.

So enjoy laughing at some of the ways commas can change everything!

Lynne Truss

Slow, children crossing.

Slow children crossing.

"Go, get him doctors!"

"Go get him, doctors!"

Every day, Anthony turns, slides, and swings.

Every day, Anthony turns slides and swings.

After we left Grandma, Mommy and I
skipped about in the park.

After we left, Grandma, Mommy, and I
skipped about in the park.

Becky teased the boy with the fluffy duck.

Becky teased the boy, with the fluffy duck.

Eat here, and get gas.

Eat here and get gas.

Becky walked on, her head a little higher than usual.

Becky walked on her head, a little higher than usual.

Look at that huge hot dog!

Look at that huge, hot dog!

The kids, who got ice cream, were very happy.

The kids who got ice cream were very happy.

The student, said the teacher, is crazy.

The student said the teacher is crazy.

No pushing, please.

No pushing please.

I've finally decided to cheer up, everybody!

I've finally decided to cheer up everybody!

What is this thing called, honey?

What is this thing called honey?

# WHY THESE COMMAS REALLY DO MAKE A DIFFERENCE!

**Slow, children crossing.**

The comma separates the two independent phrases *Slow* and *children crossing*.

**Slow children crossing.**

Without the comma, *slow* is an adjective that modifies *children*.

**Go, get him doctors!**

The comma separates the two independent clauses *Go* and *get him doctors*.

**Go get him, doctors!**

This comma makes *Go get him* a command directed at the doctors.

**Every day, Anthony turns, slides, and swings.**

The first comma sets off the introductory phrase *Every day*. The other commas separate the three verbs in the list.

**Every day, Anthony turns slides and swings.**

Without a comma after *turns*, the words *slides* and *swings* change from verbs to nouns.

**After we left Grandma, Mommy and I skipped about in the park.**

The comma separates the introductory clause *After we left Grandma*.

**After we left, Grandma, Mommy and I skipped about in the park.**

The first comma separates the introductory clause *After we left*. The second connects *Grandma* in a list with *Mommy and I*.

**Becky teased the boy with the fluffy duck.**

Without a comma, *with the fluffy duck* modifies *the boy*.

**Becky teased the boy, with the fluffy duck.**

With a comma separating the two phrases, *with the fluffy duck* describes Becky's action.

**Eat here, and get gas.**

The comma separates the two independent clauses *Eat here* and *and get gas*.

**Eat here and get gas.**

With no comma, this sentence implies one action causes the other.

**Becky walked on, her head a little higher than usual.**

The comma makes *her head a little higher than usual* modify *Becky*.

**Becky walked on her head a little higher than usual.**

With the comma after *head*, the phrase *a little higher than usual* modifies the independent clause *Becky walked on her head*.

**Look at the huge hot dog!**

Without a comma, *huge* modifies *hot dog*.

**Look at the huge, hot dog!**

Adding the comma makes *huge* and *hot* coordinating adjectives that both modify *dog*.

**The kids, who got ice cream, were very happy.**

The commas set off information that is not essential to the meaning of the sentence.

**The kids who got ice cream were very happy.**

Without commas, *who got ice cream* applies to only certain kids.

**The student, said the teacher, is crazy.**

The commas sets off the dependent clause *said the teacher*.

**The student said the teacher is crazy.**

Without commas, the student is the one making the statement.

**No pushing, please.**

The comma separates the two independent phrases *No pushing* and *please*.

**No pushing please.**

With no comma, *please* becomes a noun.

**I've finally decided to cheer up, everybody!**

The comma separates the independent clause *I've finally decided to cheer up* from *everybody*, which notes who the sentence is addressing.

**I've finally decided to cheer up everybody!**

With no comma, *everybody* becomes the object of *cheer up*.

**What is this thing called, honey?**

The comma separates the independent clause *What is this thing called* from the person being addressed, *honey*.

**What is this thing called honey?**

Without a comma, *honey* is the object of *called*.

To Georgina and Harriet
—L. T.

Thank you to Fran Rametta of Angiers Elementary School, Newton, Massachusetts, and the
teachers of Santa Cruz Catholic School, Tucson, Arizona, for help with the comma explanations.

G. P. PUTNAM'S SONS A division of Penguin Young Readers Group. Published by The Penguin Group. Penguin Group (USA) Inc., 375 Hudson Street, New York, NY 10014, U.S.A. Penguin Group (Canada), 90 Eglinton Avenue East, Suite 700, Toronto, Ontario, Canada M4P 2Y3 (a division of Pearson Penguin Canada Inc.).Penguin Books Ltd, 80 Strand, London WC2R 0RL, England. Penguin Ireland, 25 St. Stephen's Green, Dublin 2, Ireland (a division of Penguin Books Ltd.). Penguin Group (Australia), 250 Camberwell Road, Camberwell, Victoria 3124, Australia (a division of Pearson Australia Group Pty Ltd). Penguin Books India Pvt Ltd, 11 Community Centre, Panchsheel Park, New Delhi - 110 017, India. Penguin Group (NZ), Cnr Airborne and Rosedale Roads, Albany, Auckland 1310, New Zealand (a division of Pearson New Zealand Ltd). Penguin Books (South Africa) (Pty) Ltd, 24 Sturdee Avenue, Rosebank, Johannesburg 2196, South Africa. Penguin Books Ltd, Registered Offices: 80 Strand, London WC2R 0RL, England.

Published simultaneously in Canada. Manufactured in China by South China Printing Co. Ltd. Design by Gina DiMassi. Text set in Handwriter bold. Library of Congress Cataloging-in-Publication Data   Truss, Lynne. Eats, shoots & leaves : why, commas really do make a difference! / Lynne Truss ; illustrated by Bonnie Timmons.   p. cm.   1. English language—Punctuation—Juvenile literature. 2. Comma—Juvenile literature. I. Title: Eats, shoots and leaves. II. Timmons, Bonnie, ill. III. Title.   PE1450.T753 2006   428.2—dc22   2005028559   ISBN 0-399-24491-3

1 3 5 7 9 10 8 6 4 2

First Impression